Inconvenient
SKIN

nayêhtâwan wasakay

Inconvenient
SKIN

nayêhtâwan wasakay

Shane.L.Koyczan

THEYTUS BOOKS
Indig Lits

Library and Archives Canada Cataloguing in Publication

Title: Inconvenient skin = nayêhtâwan wasakay / Shane L. Koyczan.
Other titles: nayêhtâwan wasakay
Names: Koyczan, Shane L., 1976- author. | Koyczan, Shane L., 1976- Inconvenient skin. | Koyczan, Shane L., 1976- Inconvenient skin. Cree.
Description: "Cree translation provided by Solomon Ratt ; artwork by Kent Monkman, Joseph M. Sánchez, Jim Logan, Nadia Kwandibens."--Page 4 of cover. | Poems in English followed by Cree translation.
Identifiers: Canadiana 2018902917X | ISBN 9781926886510 (hardcover)
Classification: LCC PS8621.O978 I53129 2019 | DDC C811/.6â€"dc23

Cree translation by: Solomon Ratt
Cover art: Kent Monkman

THEYTUS BOOKS
www.theytus.com

On behalf on Theytus Books, we would like to acknowledge the financial support of the Government of Canada through the Book Publishing Industry Development Program (BPIDP) for our publishing activities and the Canada Council for the Arts.

We acknowledge the support of the Province of British Columbia through the British Columbia Arts Council.

We also acknowledge the support of First Peoples' Cultural Council in making the publication of *Inconvenient Skin* possible.

Printed in Canada.

Contents

Inconvenient Skin

2017 was a polarizing year for Canada. While we celebrated 150 years as a nation we have also come face to face with our own dark history. I've spent the past few years reconnecting with my father, who has had firsthand experience with residential schools. There has been a vast expanse of silence to traverse, and I'm only now discovering these missing chapters from my own origin. My hope is that this piece will continue the conversation. One of the things I've learned through this process is something about healing. To heal a wound you must first clean it... which is perhaps the most painful part. To clean a wound you must expose it to the stinging air. That is where we are right now; witnesses to the blood and pain. We face it now to heal it, or ignore it... letting the infection deepen and spread. Whichever path we choose the truth will not waiver. The cure will take as long as the sickness, and the sickness isn't yet over.

1

150 years is not so long
that the history can be forgot

pêyakwâw mitâtahtomitanaw mîna niyânanomitanaw askîwina
namôya osâm kinwêsk kâ-pê-ispayik ka-wanikiskisihk

not so long that

forgiveness can be bought with empty apologies

or unkept promises

2

namôya osâm kinwêsk êkosi

pônêyihtamowin ka-atâwêhk kwanta kâsînamâsowina ohci

âhpô êkâ kâ-kaskihtâhk asotamâkêwina

sharpened assurances that this is now

how it is

take it on good faith

and accept it

3

ê-kâsisik kêhcinâ-itwêwina mêkwâc

kâ-ispayik

ka-tâpowakêyihtamahk

ka-ohtinamahk

4

except that

history repeats itself

like someone not being listened to

mâka pîhtaw

kah-kihtwâm âh-ispayin kâ-pê-isi-pimâtisihk

tâpiskôc awiyak êkâ ê-natohtawiht

like an entire people not being heard

5

tâpiskôc kahkiaw iyiniwak êkâ ê-natohtawihcik

the word of god is hard to swallow

when good faith becomes a barren gesture

6

manitow otitwêwin âyiman ta-kitâpayihtahk

ispîhk tâpowakêyihtamowin kiyâm ê-mêtawahkêhk

7

there were men of good faith

robbing babies from their cradles

like the monsters we used to tell each other about

âtiht nâpêwak kâ-kî-pê-tâpowakêyihtahkik

kî-kimotiwak oskawâsisa tihkinâkanihk ohci

tâpiskôc wihtikowak kâ-kî-âh-âcimostâtoyâhk

8

ripping children out of their mother's arms
to be imprisoned in the houses of a god
whose teachings were love

ê-maskahktêcik oskawâsisa okâwîwâwa ospitoniyiwahk ohci
ta-kipahomiht omanitowikamikohk
manitow kâ-kiskinwahamâkêt sâkihitowin

9

did no one hear?
did god mumble?

god said love

namôya cî awiyak ê-kî-pêhtahk?
ê-kî-sakamotêyaniwêt cî manitow?

manitow kî-itwêw sâkihitowin

I had a sister – They took her away
from me. I let go of her hand.
It was the last time I'd touch her.
But I didn't know it then.....

but the things that were done
were not love

10

mâka ôma kâ-kî-itahkamikahk
namôya êwako sâkihitowin

our nation is built above the bones
of a genocide

11

kipêyakôskânêsiwininaw kî-pê-ohpikan
ka-mîscihihcik iyiniwak

12

it was not love that pried apart these families

namôya anima sâkihitowin kâ-pahkwaciwêpahikocik pêyakôskânak it is not love that abandons its treaties

namôya anima sâkihitowin kâ-nakatahk ostêsimâwasinahikana

it is not love to not acknowledge these atrocities
         to allow teenagers to freeze to death
after having been driven past city limits
and set loose to walk back in the winter cold

namôya anima sâkihitowin êkâ kâ-nâkatokâtamihk ôhi kitimâkihiwêwina
        ka-pakitinihcik oskâyak ta-nipahâskaticik
ispî kâ-otâpahihcik sisonê-ôtênâhk
êkota kâ-nakatihcik ta-ati-mostohtêcik ôtênâhk isi kâ-pipohk

15

it is not love

when an entire culture is told

stop whining

by a country still lining its pockets

with the profits of these broken promises

namôya anima sâkihitowin

ispîhk ka-wihtamâhcik iyiniwak

ka-pôni-sîsîkocik

ôhi kihc-okimâwowin kêyâpic kâ-sôniyâhkâkocik

kayâs kiyâski-otasotamâkêwiniwâwa ohci

16

this is not love

namôya ôma sâkihitowin

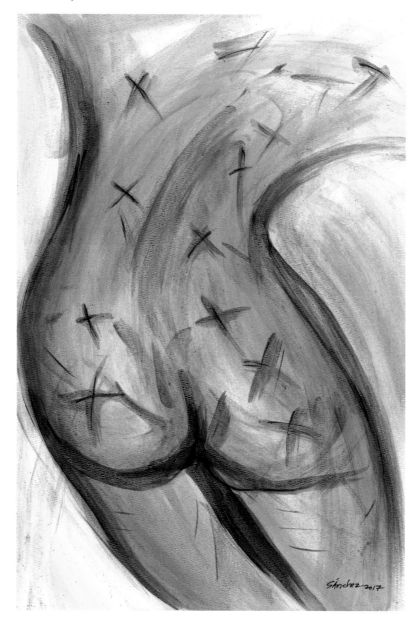

yet this is what's been done since before year one

mâka êkosi ôma ê-pê-itôtahkik aspin nistam ohci kâ-nakiskâtohk

18

150 years
is just us putting birthday candles
on top of smallpox blankets, teen suicides
and missing murdered women

pêyakwâw mitâtahtomitanaw mîna niyânanomitanaw askîwina kâ-tipiskahk
kanakî ê-astâyahk tipiskamowin-wâsaskocênikanisa
tahkohc mis-ômikîwin-akohpihk, oskâya-nisiwanâcihisowin
mîna kâ-wanihihcik kâ-nipahihcik iskwêwak

19

we can't spin our history
into something easy to accept because it isn't

it should never be

namôya ka-kî-pê-âcimisonaw
tâpiskôc ta-wihcasik ta-tâpwêhtamihk ayisk namôya wihcasin

namôya wihkâc êkosi takî-isi-ayâk

we are not free to shed our history
like an inconvenient skin

namôya ka-kî-pihkohitonaw kâ-pê-ispayik
tâpiskôc ê-pihtopayiyahk ahtay kâ-mâyâtahk

21

we are not free to turn our backs on the children
still swallowing the hollowness of poverty

namôya ka-kî-pihkohitonaw ka-kwêskikâpawêstawâyahkik awâsisak
kiyâpic ê-kitâpayihtâcik kâ-wîhpâk kitimâkisiwin

this nation is not so sturdy

that it can sustain the weight of this blind spot in our memory

ôma pêyakôskânêsiw namôya êkwayikohk maskawâw

ta-pimohtatât kosikwana anima kâ-âkôkêhohk kikiskisiwininaw

23

as Canadians
we want to live up to what we believe ourselves to be

Canadians kâ-ititoyahk
kinohtê-kwayaskokâpawîstânaw kâ-itêyimisoyahk

24

live up to each quality we value

kind

compasssionate

honest

true

strong

free

ka-nîpawîstamahk anima kâ-tâpwêyihtamahk

miyotêhêwin

kisêwâtisiwin

kwayaskitâtisiwin

tâpwêwin

sôhkitêhêwin

tipêyimisowin

25

if we ever become
who we hope we are
it will be because we see how far there is still to go
and we know that if we are not these things to everyone
then we are none of these things

kîspin wihkâc wâpamisoyahki
kâ-nohtê-isi-pimâtisiyahk
êkospî anima ayisk ê-wâpahtamahk wahyaw kiyâpic kita-itohtêyahk
êkwa mîna kikiskêyihtênaw kîspin namôya omisi kitisi-kitâpamikawinaw
namôya êkosi kitisi-ayânaw

if the world brings a challenge to one of us

it brings it to us all

we rise and fall together

26

kîspin pêyak kiyânaw kinakiskênaw mawinêhotowin

êkosi kahkiyaw kimawinêhokawinaw

kimâmawi-nîpawinaw âhpô kimâmawi-pahkisininaw

the winds of change

do not show up in our weather reports

and yet they blow from sea to sea

we stand on guard for thee

kâ-kâh-kwîskiyowêk

namôya nôkwan ita kâ-âtotamihk kâ-isiwêpahk

âta yôtin kihcikamihk ohci isko kotak kihcikamihk

nitasawêkâpawinân kiya ohci

28

funny

how those standing up for the water, the land

and everything that sustains us

are told to stand aside

are told to make way for progress

wawiyatêyihtâkwan

aniki kâ-asawêpâstahkik nipiy, askiy

êkwa kahkiyaw kîkway kâ-pimâcihikoyahk

itikawiwak kita-êkatêkâpawick

itikawiwak kita-êkatêkâpawihstahkik yahkohtêwin

we dress the future in such a pretty word
but without balance
these two wings of this same bird
cannot achieve flight

kikitâpâhtênaw ôtê nîkân tâpiskôc ka-miywâsik
mâka kîspin nama-kîkway mînopayiwin astêw
ôhi mitahtâkwana pêyakwan piyêsîs ohci
namôya kika-kaskihtânaw kita-pimihâyahk

we hop about on the ground like a wounded sparrow

kikâh-kwâskohcinisinaw mohcik tâpiskôc miswâkaniwipiyêsîs

31

our fight is not meant to be with each other
our fight is to be better
always improving
moving toward what we wish this nation to be

we can be better

ôma kâ-mâsihtâyahk namôya takî-mâsihitoyahk
ôma ohci kâ-mâsihtâyahk nawac ka-ati-miyohtêyahk
kâkikê ka-ati-miyohtêyahk
ê-nâtamahk anima kâ-isi-nitawêyihtamahk kipêyakôskânêsiwinaw

nawac ki-kakî-moyohtânaw

I would see her in
the girls play area
—sometimes all alone
I would call over
to her
Sometimes she would
wave and smile
Sometimes she wouldn't
I was wondering what was
happening to her—someone
told me she was not well
I wanted to reach over
and hug her . . .
But it wasn't allowed

32

we are a nation of neighbours who help neighbours

we are thinkers with hearts

we are feelers

we are problem solvers

and healers

kiyânaw pêyakôskânêsiw ita kâ-wâh-wîcihitocik wîtapimâkanak

kiyânaw omâmitonêyihtamwak kitêhinawa ohci

kiyânaw kimôsihtânaw

kiyânaw kinihtâ-mînahikânaw

mîna kinanâtawihowânaw

and sometimes the medicine we need most
comes from remembering who we were

so we can reconcile it against who we wish to become

êkwa âskaw anima maskihkiy nawac kâ-nitawêyihtamahk
pê-ispayin itê kâ-ohci-kiskisiyahk awîniki kiyânaw

êkosi kika-mînosihtânaw itê kâ-isi-nohtê-isi-ayâyahk

like an anthem giving rise to a tide

these shores have been missing

like the vanishing languages of a stolen people

tâpiskôc kihci-nikamowin ê-pêciciwanihkêhk

êwakonik wâsakâma kî-kwîtawîyihtâkwana

tâpiskôc kâ-wanipayiyiki opîkiskwêwiniwâwa kâ-kimotinihcik iyiniwak

a nation forced to abandon their own good faith
beneath the steeple of a god who said love

36

pêyakôskânêsiw ê-kaskimiht ta-nakatahk otâpowakêyihtamiwâw
sîpâ okiskinawâciyihk manitow kâ-itwet sâkihitowin

I don't know the future
but l have read enough of history
to see patterns in its tapestry

37

namôya nikiskêyihtên ôtê nîkân
mâka nahêyikohk nikî-ayamihtân âcimowin kâ-pê-ispayik
ta-wâpahtamân kâ-wî-isi-ayâk

38

I have seen resolve forged in adversity
and the voices we hear now
were once just seeds
that silence scattered amid a tangle of weeds
meant to strangle them away from sunlight

nikî-wâpahtên nahêyihtamowin ê-âpatahk ta-nôtinitotâkêhk
êkwa pîkiskwîwina kâ-pêhtamahk anohc
kayâs êwakoni kiscikânisa piko
kâmwâtan kî-misiwêskam miswêskamihk
takî-kipohtahikocik awasîw wâsêskwanihk ohci

but some things fight the dark for so long
that they learn to grow inside of a shadow
and they are idle no more

mâka âtiht kîkway mâsihtâw kaski-tipiskâw kinwêsk
mêtoni ê-ati-nihtâ-ohpikihki cikâstêsininâhk
êkwa namôya awasimê kihtimisinwak

40

at the core of our values
is dignity

ita kâ-mâwaci-isi-ayâyahk
kistêyimitowin astêw

and yet we strip mine a culture of its identity

mâka kiyâpic kimônahawânak iyiniwak otisîhcikêwiniwâw ohci

42

allow our leaders to erode each treaty
and stab flags into the land
as if mountains can be owned

ê-pakitinâyahkik nitokimâhkâninawak ta-nipahahkik ostêsimâwasinahikana
êkwa ta-cimatâcik wêwêpâscikana askîhk
tâpiskôc waciya takî-tipêyihcikâtêki

as if water is property

tâpiskôc nipiy takî-tipêyihcikâtêk

44

where is our dignity
if we cannot hold true to the promises we make?

tâniwê kikistêyimisowinaw
kîspin êkâ ê-kî-itôtamahk kâ-isi-asotamâtitoyahk

what value does our word have

if all it ever does is break?

tânisi mâka takî-isi-sôhkêyihtamahk kitasotamâtowininawa

ispîhk kapê êkâ ê-nâkatawêyihtamahk

46

the choices we make today
will be felt across time

anima kâ-itôtamahk anohc
kika-ispayistamowânawak ôtê nîkân

their consequences inherited

not by the echoes of who we were

but by the children our examples have taught

kika-âsôskamawânawak kitâniskô-wâhkômâkaninawak

namôya wiya cîstâwêsiniwin kâ-pê-isi-ayâyahk

mâka awâsisak aniki kâ-pê-isi-kiskinwawâpamikoyahkik

48

what future will they have
if our only gift to them
are the lessons we forgot?

tânisi mâka kâ-wî-isi-pimâtisicik ôtê nîkân
kîspin kimêkiwina piko anihi
kîkwaya kâ-wanikiskisiyahk.

Shane.L.Koyczan

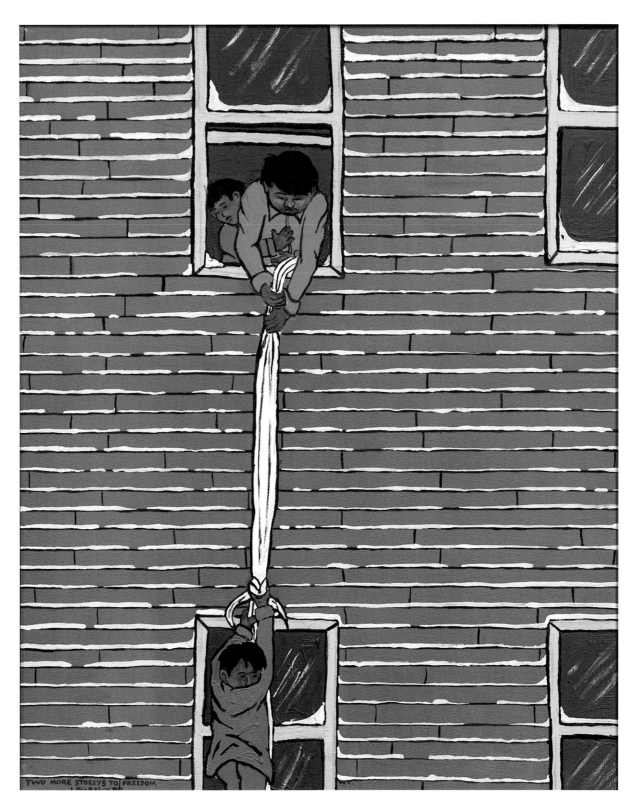

List of Works

List of Works

Biographies

Shane Koyczan, writer, poet, spoken word artist was born in Yellowknife, NWT (1976) and grew up in Penticton, BC. Koyczan went to Okanagan University College where he studied creative writing. There, his writing professor suggested that he should focus on poetry rather than fiction, launching Koyczan's future in spoken word. He is a co-founder of the spoken word "talk rock" trio Tons of Fun University (TOFU), and has performed around the globe at universities and at music and literary festivals. His writing and performance is vital, witty and sincere: he reaches the hearts of his audiences with his powerful verses and has brought the Canadian spoken word movement to the international stage.

Visiting Hours (2005) is Shane Koyczan's first book, and was selected as one of the books of the year by the Guardian (UK) and the Globe and Mail. Followed by *Stick Boy* (2008) a novel in free verse that surveys the misery of being bullied and the reversal of taking that pain and inflicting it on others. Shane Koyczan won the 2004 CBC Radio *Poetry Face-Off*, and is the first non-American poet to win the US National Individual Poetry Slam. His work was featured on *Heart of a Poet*, a documentary series produced by filmmaker Maureen Judge and aired on Bravo television. Koyczan was commissioned by the Canadian Tourism Commission to write a poem, *We Are More*, which has been performed across the country, including at the opening of the 2010 Winter Olympic Games in Vancouver, BC. Koyczan has been featured on CBC, NPR, BBC, and ABC (Australia) radio.

https://shanekoyczan.com

Biographies

Joseph Sánchez has a unique place in the Canadian First Nations art movement. Born and raised in Arizona, Joseph lived in Canada in the 1970s and was a founding member of the Professional Native Indian Artists Association alongside Daphne Odjig, Alex Janvier, Norval Morrisseau and others. Known as both an artist and curator, Joseph's vast list of achievements include Director and Chief Curator of the Institute of American Indian Arts in Santa Fe, New Mexico.

www.josephmsanchez.com

Jim Logan was born in 1955 in New Westminster, BC and studied at the Kootenay School of Art in Nelson, BC. Since 1984 he has exhibited his works in over forty venues. Much of his oeuvre is characterised by his many novel approaches to the narrative of Native life from folksy, illustrative work to his current use of erudite parody. In either case, Logan's humour and affection for his culture is tempered by a concern for the restoration of identity and self-awareness within First Nations communities.

Logan laments the low visibility of Aboriginal aesthetics in formal art history and uses parody to underscore the hegemony of Western artistic tradition. Thus by "Indianizing" the masters, old and new, he has added new significance, a Native perspective, to the icons of Western art. Logan's essentially post-modern approach in delivering a message through his art is therefore a "questioning of European dominance in all aspects of our culture, not just throughout North America, but the world as well. This general acceptance of European culture as a positive force, an ideal to aspire to and attain... I started questioning how I've been affected by this, and how my people have been affected by this."

www.jim-logan.net

Biographies

Nadya Kwandibens is Anishinaabe (Ojibwe) from the Animakee Wa Zhing #37 First Nation in Northwestern Ontario. She is a self-taught portrait and events photographer and has travelled extensively across Canada for over 10 years. In 2008 she founded Red Works Photography. Red Works is a dynamic photography company empowering contemporary Indigenous lifestyles and cultures through photographic essays, features, and portraits. Red Works specializes in natural light portraiture and headshots sessions plus event and concert photography. Red Works also provides image licensing, workshops, presentations and print products. Nadya's photography has been exhibited in group and solo shows across Canada and the United States.

In addition to commissioned works, Nadya delivers empowering photography workshops and presentations for youth, universities, and community groups. She resides in the traditional territory of the Anishinaabe in Northwestern Ontario.

https://www.redworks.ca/

Biographies

Kent Monkman is a Canadian artist of Cree ancestry who is well known for his provocative reinterpretations of romantic North American landscapes. Themes of colonization, sexuality, loss, and resilience—the complexities of historic and contemporary Indigenous experience, are explored in a variety of mediums, including painting, film/video, performance, and installation.

His glamorous gender fluid alter-ego Miss Chief Eagle Testickle appears in much of his work as a time travelling, shape shifting and supernatural being, who reverses the colonial gaze, upending received notions of history and Indigenous people. With Miss Chief at centre stage, Monkman has created memorable site specific performances at the McMichael Canadian Art Collection, The Royal Ontario Museum, The Smithsonian's National Museum of the American Indian, Compton Verney, and most recently at the Denver Art Museum. Monkman has been awarded the Egale Leadership Award (2012), the Indspire Award (2014), the Hnatyshyn Foundation Visual Arts Award (2014), the Bonham Centre Award (2017), an honorary doctorate degree from OCAD University (2017) and the Premier's Award for Excellence in the Arts (2017).

His work has been exhibited internationally and is widely represented in the collections of major museums in Canada and the USA. He is represented by Pierre-François Ouellette art contemporain in Montreal and Toronto and Trepanier Baer Gallery in Calgary.

http://www.kentmonkman.com/